Forgetfulness

By the Same Author from Shearsman Books

Anonymous Intruder
Shifting Registers
Makers of Empty Dreams
Identity Papers
New York Hotel
The Underground Cabaret
Night Window

Bitter Grass
(translated from the Italian of Gëzim Hajdari)

Ian Seed

Forgetfulness

Shearsman Books

First published in the United Kingdom in 2026 by
Shearsman Books Ltd
PO Box 4239
Swindon
SN3 9FN

Shearsman Books Ltd Registered Office
30–31 St. James Place, Mangotsfield, Bristol BS16 9JB
(this address not for correspondence)

www.shearsman.com

ISBN 978-1-83738-011-4

Acknowledgements

My thanks to the editors of the following publications, where some of these poems first appeared, sometimes in different versions:

Anthropocene, Berlin lit, Blackbox Manifold, The Café Irreal, The Friday Poem, Hinterland Magazine, I Remember (a Red Ceilings limited-edition pamphlet), *Litter, Long Poem Magazine, Noon: A Journal of Short Poetry, Notes on Literature: For Readers and Writers (*University of Chester), *Scattering My Mother's Ashes* (a Red Ceilings limited-edition pamphlet), *Shearsman* magazine, *Stride, Talking about Strawberries All of the Time, Tears in the Fence*, and *The Tuesday Poem.*

Alcatraz, eds Cassandra Atherton & Paul Hetherington (Gazebo Books, 2022)

Infinite thanks to Tony Frazer.

Contents

Alors, j'étouffai des sanglots d'humiliation et j'écrivis cette page-ci, mais avec beaucoup plus de littérature ridicule.

—Max Jacob

For Justyna and Chiara

1

Scattering My Mother's Ashes

1

In the village hall, a man with learning difficulties is reading out a poem he has written. 'What's the point of writing in that silly way?' my mother wants to know. She looks out of a window at the cows. They are of a rare breed, much smaller and more delicate than ordinary cows. 'So pretty, yet soon they will no longer be here,' she says. And here is my father at the door, buying raffle tickets. I haven't seen him since he died. He won't know of all the changes that have taken place since then.

2

Waiting to cross the street, I saw my mother go by in a coach. She was at the back on her own, staring out of the window. I ran after the coach, waving, and caught up with it at some traffic lights. I put my hands together in a begging gesture and the driver let me on.

My mother was glad to see me, but not quite sure who I was. She told me she was on her way to Portugal to visit her youngest son. I didn't tell her she was on the coach to Birmingham, the city where I was born.

At the next stop, the door at the back opened, and stayed open even when we set off again. The driver must have forgotten to close it. I had to hold my mother tight when we went around a corner.

3

Now that I'd quit my job at the university, I had plans to go to Milan and hang out with an old poet friend there. My colleagues wished me well in my retirement, even though I'd told them I wasn't retiring; I was dropping out of the system, resting for a week or two, then setting off on new adventures before I developed dementia like my mother.

A fortnight later I was in Milan, the wind sweeping down the dark, deserted street where the bus had dropped me off. There was no sign of the poet who'd promised to meet me, but after a while I heard someone softly singing. A young man, who looked like a student I'd once known, emerged from the darkness. I wanted to ask him the way, but when he saw me he drew back, and no words would come to me.

4

Catching a glimpse of myself in a waiting-room mirror, I saw what looked like a black cherry on the lower lid of each eye. I thought perhaps they were enormous sties. Yet they'd appeared out of nowhere and didn't hurt when I touched them. They made me think of trapped, bruised tears. If I pressed harder, would they burst? What kind of mess would they leave behind?

5

Not too long now till we reach the top, I tell myself. We are pausing for a rest on some mossy rocks in the cold sunshine. I feel like a stranger among family and friends, many of whom I haven't seen for years. We've come together to scatter my mother's ashes. A little further up is a small plateau with a café. I'm desperate to be on my own, just for a few minutes, so I offer to get hot drinks. There follows an astonishingly complicated series of requests. Everybody wants something different. By the time I reach the café, the only order I remember – perhaps because it was the last I was given – is a *cocoa, made with half-milk, lactose-free, and half-water, with one and a half lumps of light-brown sugar*. In front of the unsmiling woman at the till, I find myself unable to speak. A young man walks in. It takes a moment for me to recognise him as the son of one of my cousins; he has three small children of his own now. Seeing the look on my face, he offers to help with the orders. He remembers them all even though he wasn't really paying attention, he tells me, with his hearty smile. 'We'll be at the top in no time,' he says.

6

I was walking down the street when I saw a little old man rolling on the pavement and weeping. It was only when I bent down to see if I could help him that one or two people stopped to see what was going on. The man recovered quickly once he had our attention – he said he'd eaten something that didn't agree with him.

Later I saw him outside a church, again rolling on the ground, but this time with louder, angrier sobs. When he saw the weary expression on my face, he began to cry even louder.

'Don't you realise we all have something to weep about?' I said.

'Yes,' he said, 'there is so much to weep about in this town, isn't there?'

I didn't tell him my mother had died; I hadn't yet found the heart to weep.

7

Half a year on from my mother's death, not knowing which way to turn, I rang a Christian helpline. A woman asked me my name, and then in a gentle, yet matter-of-fact tone told me I had ten minutes at most because someone else might be waiting on the line. I found this oddly reassuring – I wasn't the only one who was feeling lost and it meant I wouldn't have to talk to her for very long.

'Well,' I said, feeling silly, 'I'm just curious to know a bit more about what it's like to repent and become a Christian.'

'I understand,' she said softly, in a practical way adding, 'There are many like you, afraid to admit their need.'

'But all that dogma,' I blurted out, 'how can anyone believe such nonsense?'

'No one is asking you to believe anything, just to have faith, which means to be open one step at a time.'

I felt then that within the granted minutes I had infinite time, because love was infinite, and all I had to do was accept it.

8

It was the last day of my employment. My father turned up at the campus Woodland Festival in an old two-seater sports car, roof down, driving recklessly (as he always had) through a stream right up to where I was sitting with some colleagues round a picnic cloth on the grass. He'd come to say hello, he said.

'I can't believe you're here,' I said.

I thought he'd died, though I'd heard more recently that he hadn't, just been very ill and was now recovered. In fact, he looked quite young, being much slimmer than when I'd last seen him. Perhaps we could be friends again now that my mother was no longer alive.

'I've brought a small book of poems,' he said, sitting down beside me and stretching out his long legs. He opened an old school satchel and took out half a dozen stapled pamphlets with plain-brown covers. 'Would anyone like to see them?' he asked.

'I'm sure they would,' I said. This was so different from the time when I would have been ashamed of his presence and ignored him, or even said something to remind him of past sins.

Inside the pamphlet was a series of sepia photos of my father with my mother and me as a small child, with my mother before I was born, and of my father before he'd met my mother, going back to when he was a small child himself. I couldn't find any poems, but the photos had places and dates written in the black ink of the sort once used in school inkwells.

My colleagues turned the pages idly for a few moments before putting the pamphlets down and turning their attention to the food and wine now being served. It was as if they preferred to play their roles in a rather unbelievable pastoral scene than to look at these photos, which, I realised, although genuine, were equally unreliable as a representation of reality.

9

There are just a few of us on the bare, windy hill, standing around in scattered groups. My older brother is telling me he has taken up fishing now that he has finally decided to dedicate some time to himself after years of taking care of others – our mother until she recently died, his wife, her father until he died, etc. He is almost apologetic, but also a tad defiant as he looks into the distance where the sun is shining on the meandering river. He takes another sip from the cup of tea an old lady has hobbled up the hill to bring him from the stall at the bottom. Now she is hobbling back down again. It's a miracle she doesn't fall. I run after her and ask if she'd like some help – that will give me the chance to make some kind of contribution and also to have a cup of tea myself.

A few minutes later, carrying a tray with teapot and cups, I come across an old colleague. He tells me he's had a nervous breakdown and has been sent here to recuperate. Seeing me drink yet another cup I'm meant to be distributing to others, he warns me not to have too many. 'You're hyper enough already,' he says. I realise my heart *is* beating rather fast.

I look across the slope at my brother. His cup's now empty and he's looking quite forlorn. I feel a drop of something on my cheek, and then another. I'm not the only one. All of us now are looking up at the sky – none of us had any plan for what to do if it rained today. A drop splashes into what must be my fifth cup of tea.

Forgetfulness

Walking up the mountain, I see my mother sitting on the café terrace of her new care home. She's looking remarkably young – her hair's been dyed its old dark colour and someone must have applied a lotion to make her skin all smooth again. Yet she still has that look in her eyes of not knowing where she is anymore. I doubt she will recognise me, but she greets me by name. I tell her I'm on my way to meet a friend at the top of the mountain – I can't stop for long. She nods, though I'm not sure she's understood. Deep down we both know she's no longer alive, but neither of us can bring ourselves to say so.

One night

I was woken by a tapping on the window. When I opened the curtain, I saw a small girl with her palms on the glass, other children huddled behind her. To be friendly, I placed my fingertips on the inside of the pane where hers were and tapped back. I thought of inviting them in, but it was far too late so after a few moments I closed the curtain and returned to bed. The tapping grew louder, more insistent, but I found it oddly soothing and was soon asleep again. At first light the visitors were gone, but there were holes in the glass the size of a child's fingertips and my room was much colder.

2

Untitled

dark windows   a country
never seen   old wounds
still wet   flower-headed
between frames   what other face
so stark and turning   the slope
veined where   it breaks those
who sing   the form upon us
shared with stones   drop
by drop   enter the gap
far within the other   father
whose words   lie
to hand   shadow
through   falling blades
pass   without dying

The Jugglers

1

You walk down stone steps into a crowded square.
No-one turns at your approach. They stand in small groups,
chatting, laughing, waiting for a performance about to take
    place.
It turns out to be only a set of jugglers who throw their pins
over the nothingness of our lives, maiming the air with their cries.

2

The tricks they showed us looked cheap and flashy,
but they could be life-changing, we were told, if only
one understood their significance. But none of us ever did.
And that was the point perhaps. We watched them perform more
out of courtesy than anything else. Funny
how we can be conned into doing something
we don't really want to do just to avoid giving offence. We believe
it's just for a while, but it ends being a lifetime. And simply
because we believe there is no-one we can turn to
for an alternative vision.

3

When the show is over, the audience feel such passion
they decide to re-enact it. They themselves become the actors
or at least genuine copies of them.

4

It was past midnight. I was returning to my hotel.
I thought I was alone when I crossed the main square
but a man emerged from the shadows and took my hand.
He led me down alleyways to the banks of the river.
I fell asleep in his arms under the stars.
In the morning he was gone, but he left
the shape of his body in the grass.

5

Fingertips reach the tender inside
beyond mere greeting and passing away.
This breath on my face, on my trembling
shoulder blades, the small part of me
which is still open, left over from the wound,
the only place you can enter.

6

It isn't me he's after but my double, vanishing beside me
in the art of dying until he is no more than a fuzzy outline
on a hazy day in which the sun has become unbearably hot.

7

Now I've come to a door, but if I knock
it will lead to a series of commitments.
Like being caught in a maze
where one turning commits you to another
but you can't find the exit
where someone – you don't know who – is waiting.

8

I am sitting in the bus station writing a letter to you.
And then there you are in the sunlight in front of me.
'But what are you doing in this country?' I ask
almost as if I were disappointed to see you.
You smile with pained eyes.
'I've crossed a continent to find you –
when will you embrace me?'

9

Wouldn't it be wonderful, I asked you
in my dream, if we could meet again
and act as if our lives hadn't taken place
since the last time?
But you said we needed to go beyond
regret into a kind of dance which in some
measure both contained and overcame that regret.

10

The road is made of stones and stories. It merges
with the light ahead. It has mapped
our dreams. How long shall we linger
on its verge, nursing our cut feet, gazing
with affection at old scars?

Transfigure

Easy to slip from the question itself
to new facts, to panes that reflect
the you, the blur of you: the unquiet
smiling, duplicated you, almost eroded,
the eye leaking a suspended tear.
If instead we stay inside the asking,
a fictional window opens, a prospect
emerges which is more than a reworking
of an old map. Each step is the first
on an unmade path towards a horizon
whose mystery remains unreached.
In the unwrinkled pages of the story
the end is uncertain, is forever
in the making, and only possibly true.

Office at Night

You're my hurricane in stockings, you say.
Through the window presses the sound
of a sentimental strain, situating our embrace

somewhere outside in the dark-drenched
beauty of the city. *You're my moony*
hoodlum, you say, *never mind the ones*

who would tell us not to risk it all
with our escapade. It starts to rain, the rain
grows heavy. Through the downpour

we can see pale faces, legs, particles
of street light. *Our dream's already*
come halfway true, you want me

to believe just this once. Shall I
humour you? Soon we'll be tramping
wet pavements. It's true you have

your moments of realism, despair even,
yet your heartbeat insists, penetrates
my silence, with its illusion of no pain.

Roles

Folded, cold, in thick disguise, she shakes
her head, bends over him, where he has taken
residence on the path, eyes half-closed:
'I do not kiss statues. There will be

no more garden. You must learn to
welcome me, you who are deep in dreams.'
I run downstairs, not touching the banisters,
following her following him deeper

into the garden, now full of dry, split
leaves, some floating by in the current
of an icy stream, their sorrow pulled away
under a mossy bridge. He has crossed

to the other side. There remains
only the story of the way, where we lose
ourselves in the spaces as they appear
slipping through our fingers, open and bright.

Tenants

This betrayal does not mean my promise
did not exist. You take the key, still there
under the stone by the back door. Lost
among the lumber we turn defenceless,

make a search of the room again. A fly's
flickering against the window testifies
to its dream of elsewhere. In dim light
you kiss me, in this place we have entered

so rashly. The slant sun's silvering
dismantles our memories. In your breath
in the cold, is a picture of the world.
There's a feeling of something different

on the other side, where every piece
of the story would fit, where from cut
to cut the stills of the film of our lives
would become like our tears believable.

Wakening

Deep on our island, we dream of being
discovered by a long and perilous route.
It never ends: the sea journey, the story
told just for the darkness, even if later

nothing adds up at the edge of the waves.
Before us dissolves the boundary where
water meets land. Our lives no longer have
a shape, only an endless stretching away.

The more we speak of them, the less real
they seem. The old times have to wait,
though the same report, the means of return,
line our faces. They can only deepen

like a final judgment from a distance
which closes. Yet at sunrise, voyagers may
emerge in a slow light beyond the brink
while the water breathes at our feet.

Self-help

It seems it's she who's died to heal his private world
and her fingers know the colour of his eyes, lucrative
as they present themselves under a pale sky
as if in apology for being good. She'd found him

on a bench crying for the life that'd oozed away
in a time once bright and quick, with a good dose
of pretty tipple, self-confidence around the mouth,
a pleasure to be a part of, but she never heard

or felt him enter, warm as a sunned cat. Acting
was her teenage dream, but can she now play mother
as she reaches in her bag for something for his smoker's
cough? This musing makes me feel like my lighter self,

she explained, the corners of her mouth trembling.
It'll still be warm when she returns in the morning,
wet from a night of it, heavy in her black dress.
The cock can tell the weather's going to change.

Trick-kissed

You push through, finding yourself behind the curtains,
the earliest of the party. It turns out to be a walk of shame.
Consider yourself a stranger in this country. Wait until the end
of the act of secret gratification, at the appointed hour

with the very same man you say you love, a man silhouetted,
with the worst of faces, continually passing in the street
but you don't love him enough. Nerves surge, to be sure.
He comes closer to ease the business. Why not?

The girl at the bar was found to be dislocated, still
so obedient. She has an amazing body actually, already
burning the stranger and with the pressing, if passionless,
invitation of the curve of her breasts, he has entangled himself

so far as to undress her soft, fine fabric in the cheerfullest
manner, if without much deftness. And what are you doing?
Frying peaches in butter! C'est drôle, c'est vrai. She's wet
with a jolt, and her tears when they fall are swift and bright.

Shush

I see my weakness, most unseemly
the emptiness between four walls, and
my culpability. Have mercy on me,
humble door, where humanity

has passed like smoke. Hello, yellow bird.
I raise my face to the sky. It seems it is
singing to me. My days will change. I've lost
my regrets and complicated desires.

There's a hole here. Who am I? There's
little left except a grown man in a dark
suit crying in public. The idea of death.
I don't know what these people think. Come on,

I'm not afraid, but I would like something
to come to me from the infinite
where I can multiply. I have no mission
left to fulfil. One by one the mouths will close.

Unscripted

A heavy snow. The film eyes
of a stranger. This street is absent
from the story of the city

which I cannot recognise, though
my body's memory can read
its twists and turns, its lines

broken through movement. The shape
of this snowflake resists
the tyranny of completion. I

is the space of the abandoned
intersection, the recorder motionless
for the first time.

Emerging Picture

1

my broom is in the corners
in a roundabout way
common features drop out
family resemblances
in the overlapping of fibres
my window overlooks
as I struggle into it
with the tips of my fingers
no one on the narrow path

2

colder and darker
the wearer's head uncovers
invisible people
snow in their mouths
where footsteps grow fainter
the same day they talk
each to his house forgiven
and I may be in them
the great body

3

why was this perfume
the silent angel's
odd shadow still scudding
its unrecognizable
scent mixed in
still loitering outside
I was ready somewhere near
in the open wherever we look
a mouthful of polar air

4

some sort of foreigner
why cry I wonder
my face wet with snow
as if there were two of us
pushed in amongst the whiteness
my own trembling lips
still drinking
what else to call him
but the breath that has been

Untested

each night this distance
    to cross between contours

    this unbreathing silence
these eyes without colour

    this fall
through shadows of clouds

morning, bring promise
    of ground beneath my window

3

Avanti

The woman next to me on the train needs some extra space to breastfeed her baby, so I decide to take a walk to stretch my legs. Wandering all the way through Second and First Class, I come to a window right at the front facing the railway tracks head on. Such an open, fast-changing view! An electronic sign informs me I can book a seat there for just £8. That will be for my next journey.

By the time I get back to my own carriage the baby has fallen asleep with its mouth around the mother's nipple. Remaining on my feet, I start to tell her about the special window, but she puts her finger to her lips. I nod, realizing how thoughtless I have been, and decide now to make my way to the back of the train, wondering if this is where the driver is located, or indeed if there is a driver at all.

Guests

In the packed hotel foyer, there's a Japanese family looking lost, but everyone is too busy to notice them. I am about to pass by when I spot the Japanese lady in a wheelchair fluttering a fan close to her wizened face. She must be almost a hundred years old.

They can hardly speak English, but they show me the card with their room number on. The lady in the wheelchair tilts her head to one side and smiles at me. I lead them to the lift, pushing the wheelchair myself through the crowd. I even get into the lift with them, press the button for their floor, and wheel her out of the lift when we arrive. She smiles again, but in a forced way, and presses her hand to her chest as if she's having trouble breathing. She points at the low ceiling of the corridor.

'Don't worry – your room will be big and bright,' I say, although I have no idea whether this is true or not, since I have only just arrived at the hotel myself.

Blonde on Blonde

In the courtroom, my Norwegian wife said I'd ruined her life. She wept copious tears, but much of this was just for the drama. More than ashamed, I was pleased by the way the magistrate looked at me with horror. I enjoyed playing the pantomime villain, for I could see he was secretly enjoying it too.

Afterwards, I accompanied her to our old home, where I kissed her goodbye on the doorstep. I was free at last to go down to the pub on my own without feeling guilty, but then I thought she might like it if I invited her to go with me one last time.

At the pub, there was a 'blonde-on-blonde' night. My hair was white now, though it had once been what my ex-wife called 'dirty blonde'. She was the only genuine blonde there, and by far and away the most beautiful woman.

The magistrate was there, too, with his blonde wig, but he hadn't even bothered to shave. His large belly swayed while he danced, beer spilling from the pint glass in his hand. Nobody would dance with him apart from me.

Literary

At end of the festival, there was much gossip around the fact that the poet P had left his wife for a man almost forty years his junior. 'I just don't get it,' said the editor E.

'But a person's identity, sexual or spiritual or otherwise, isn't fixed,' I said, 'it's more like a hog on a spit, changing what it hides or reveals as it turns in the firelight.'

The editor looked momentarily impressed, but had he understood what I was talking about?

We stopped at a table so that I could pick up the unsold copies of my books.

'That's quite a pile you've got there,' he said.

Was he referring to my having published so many books or to the fact that not many of them had sold? I chose to respond to the former.

'Oh, they're only slim volumes,' I said. 'Mind you, I've just published a thick volume of French translation, not quite in time to be represented here – *The Dice Cup* by Max Jacob, who once wrote that personality is no more than an error of persistence.'

Now the editor seemed more genuinely impressed, but said nothing because at that moment the poet P had entered the village hall and was making straight towards us.

Pastoral

after Max Jacob

The three soldiers in their red uniforms were sitting on the river bank, their long rifles laid to rest on the grass. 'Soldiers are not handsome in themselves, except they can make themselves look as if they are,' I declared from my perch on a fallen tree trunk nearby. 'People may say *that beard is ugly*, but that's only because it happens not to be in fashion at a particular time.' I looked at one of the young soldiers – slim, dark hair, blue eyes, whose name I gathered from their conversation I'd listened to earlier was Tom – and went on: 'But there are some soldiers who are extraordinarily handsome whatever they wear, whatever the fashion.' I looked at the other two soldiers. 'And you too can make yourselves handsome with just a few changes. As for me, I'm out of the game now.'

Mechanical

I wish I'd never bought that house in the village. As soon as I arrived, the next-door neighbour began to build a metal sculpture on the road in front of my gate. It grew bigger each day. I had no idea what it was supposed to be, but soon it was blocking out the light.

What's more, he kept asking me in his gruff voice to get involved and assist him. When I tried to explain that I had my writing to do, he regarded my pale, smooth hands with contempt.

As the weeks passed, I became more and more morose. The villagers, who had once been so friendly, now began to avoid me. Inevitably, the situation would lead to a showdown between me and my neighbour. Inevitably he would defeat me with his large greasy fists.

Then I would grow subservient to him, in both mind and body, and have no choice but to spend my days assisting him with his meaningless, mechanical enterprise.

Trunks

While walking in the forest, I came upon a young man stripping by the side of the path until he was in his bathing trunks. I felt envious. I would have loved an outdoor swim myself, even though there was a nip in the air. But where was he going to swim? He stepped off the path into some swampy water I hadn't noticed before because it merged so perfectly with the darkness of the trees. As he began his breaststroke, the water released a sulphurous stink, but still I would have joined him if only I'd had my trunks with me.

It Was a Cloudy Day

I was walking on my own along a ridge by the sea when I heard someone behind me. Normally this might have made me nervous and I would have turned to see who was there. This time instead I whistled a tune as loudly and clearly as I could to show whoever it was that nothing could trouble me. I grew so absorbed with trying to whistle in tune that I didn't notice the tide coming in. Then I realised that my feet were wet and I was trapped. The person behind had climbed to a higher point and seemed to be watching me, but I couldn't see the expression on their face, or even if they were a man or a woman.

Confession

The young woman – dressed as my grandmother used to in the 1920s – wouldn't stop following me through the streets of the seaside town. She followed me all the way to my hotel, then up the stairs and into my room. She said, Tell me a story, but I had no more stories left.

So I offered her a glass of wine instead, and, in order to get a bit of peace, slipped in some sleeping pills. The next morning I woke to find her stone cold beside me. How was I going to get rid of the body?

I went for a walk along the beach to think things through. When I got back, not knowing whether to hand myself in or run away, I found her shivering into wakefulness. Thank god you're alive, I said.

Why wouldn't I be? she said.

Shelter

I left the doctor's without taking the ad-hoc blood pressure test they offered because I was fed up with waiting. Besides, I'd only gone in there in the first place because it had started to rain.

On the bus home, I thought I saw my wife going into the police station, presumably also to get out of the rain, so I got off at the next stop and followed her in. The sergeant at reception told me she'd been taken to a room upstairs because she seemed lost and distraught. 'Ah, but look – here she is again,' he said, pointing to a woman coming down the stairs.

It wasn't her at all, but a thin woman with grey, straggly hair, streaked in places with faded dyed blond. I was tempted to give her a hug, just to reassure her, but then realised that wouldn't be appropriate.

When I finally did get home, my wife wasn't there, but there was a message on voicemail from the doctor's surgery. They wanted to know what had happened to me. They sounded worried and cross – more cross than worried.

January

My first day back, I couldn't find my presentation on my laptop. I couldn't even remember what it was I was supposed to be talking about. My colleagues, my boss and our potential customers watched my fumbling with growing impatience. 'I'm sorry,' I said.

A few minutes later, I found myself walking through the city in the cold mid-morning. I wanted to cry but didn't want to be seen weeping. Then, coming in the opposite direction, I saw Angelo, an old colleague I hadn't met in years. I'd heard he was some kind of artist now.

'My God, is it really you?' he said. He looked into my eyes. 'Is everything all right?'

'To tell the truth,' I said, unable to hold back the tears now, 'not today. I don't know what's happened to me.'

He reached out and put a hand on my shoulder. 'Where's home?'

'Not too far from here,' I said, though I wasn't at all sure.

'We'll find it together,' he said, putting his arm through mine.

By the time we arrived, it was almost dark. I thought of inviting him in, but I was afraid he'd refuse, or accept out of pity.

Fired

There was one poem left to workshop when the last session I was ever going to teach at the university came to the end of its allotted time. I said we could add an extra quarter of an hour for the poem, but then found myself for the first time in years dying for a cigarette. Even if smoking was of course forbidden in the seminar rooms, I asked one of the students to ask Stella in the office if she would offer me one of her cigarettes. A couple of minutes later the students watched incredulously as I lit up (with a match from the box Stella had lent me) and puffed away – like a poet from the 1970s, it occurred to me, as I began asking questions about the poem to get the students talking instead of staring.

Distraction

Since it was a sunny day, my daughter and her partner asked me to come around and look after their baby so they could go out on their own for a change. They left me rocking the baby in my arms in their front yard, wondering how long they'd be gone. After an hour or so, a man stopped by in a car. He said he'd been sent by my daughter and her partner to take me to the park to join them there. But they weren't in the park. What's more, there was no one else around, apart from my mother, or the ghost of my mother, drifting in the darkness of a patch of trees, looking like *her* mother when she was young. I was going to ask her for help, then remembered she wasn't real. Then I thought of calling my older brother and asking him what to do next, but he'd only tell me off for accepting lifts from strangers.

Choice

There's a fight in a dark passageway between a boy and a big man with a black beard and swinging belly.

The boy has been lured into the passageway. If he can outwit the man for just two minutes, the man will admit defeat, and the boy will be acquitted of any misdeeds.

But the boy could easily be killed in that time.

Now all he can do is duck and weave, or try to hide in the wet darkness of the deepest parts of the passageway, or he can try to make the man pity him, though this is unlikely to have any effect, or he can simply stand and wait, his face to one side, showing himself in all his vulnerability, turning the other cheek.

Duty

I was terminally ill, so I took their pill to die. There was no one with me – I'd said I wished to die alone. No one, that is, apart from the nurse, who was only doing her duty. I felt serene, detached but just as I was slipping away, her expressionless face came close to mine. It was only then I realised I wanted to live, to be with people I loved. I shouted *not yet, not yet, oh please not yet*, waving my arms like a man drowning, while the nurse looked on, at first with disbelief, and then with irritation, as if she were angry with herself for not completing the job properly.

Promise

Just as I'm about to take the train home, the gruff, old man I've been waiting for all day long turns up. Now I can row you across the lake, he says with a surprisingly disarming smile – all the way to that island, he adds, pointing into the distance. But by this time, I'm hungry, there are storm clouds gathering, and just a few moments ago a woman whispered to me that in reality the island was no more than a tiny rock, on which the old man and I would barely fit.

Relations

My grandfather, who had committed suicide, was in an old-fashioned train compartment with me, lying in my arms. I remembered the softness of his woollen suit from my teenage years. He was just as lost as he had been back then after my grandmother died. He was comforted by my holding him, but not sure who either of us was.

Years later

I find myself weeping with my grandfather over his death. Only now are we reconciled. We could so easily have been closer, I realise – there was no need to be mistrustful. My half-aunt, a daughter from his third marriage, is surprised, but pleased, to come upon us embracing, though she's more than a little concerned by our copious tears.

Before the Blitz

Approaching Piccadilly Circus with
my daughter's hand in mine, I remember
walking as a child by my father's side
with the same view of the fountain ahead,
and I remember him telling me that he too
had walked down this street with his
father, visiting the city in August '39.

Oxford Street

passing car –
a woman in an evening dress
rolls down the passenger window
tosses out
a burning cigarette

I want to kiss
her smoky lips

4

I Remember

(after Joe Brainard)

I remember my dad's 1930s black car with running boards. He'd inherited the car from his dad. I remember it got stuck on a humpback bridge with one of its wheels spinning over the edge.

I remember when I was four my mum sent me ahead of her down the lane with a branch in my hand to frighten away the hissing geese.

I remember jumping onto a donkey's back from a gate and riding it bareback until it stopped at a hedge and sent me flying into the next field.

I remember when I was six having a crush on a blond girl called Linda. I remember learning how to tie my shoelaces.

I remember walking to school in the snow and not wanting to arrive.

I remember a teacher in primary school used to touch us up. I don't remember his name.

I remember when 'She Loves You, Yeah, Yeah, Yeah' was number one.

I remember my mum and dad shouting in the night and the woman downstairs banging on her ceiling.

I remember going to see *A Hard Day's Night* in a Cardiff cinema. My favourite Beatle was Ringo.

I remember dancing on my own round the front room with the radio blasting out The Rolling Stones' new single 'Get Offa My Cloud'. My mum yelled at me from the kitchen to turn it down.

I remember doing *bob-a-job* for the Cubs in my green uniform, then spending the money on sweets.

I remember my mum's black eye and my uncle arriving in his van to take us away to live with him and my aunt.

I remember Kaby, our Siamese cat, roaming my uncle and aunt's large garden, where we lived in a caravan. She'd been given as a kitten to my mum and dad on their wedding day.

I remember walking across the Cardiff bay to Barry Island with my dad. My mum told him to watch out for the tides.

I remember my dad barking back at an Alsatian dog behind a steel fence.

I remember travelling to Italy with him when I was eight. He was happier on his own.

I remember we stopped by the roadside in France on our way to Italy and a grasshopper hopped into my plastic mug of tea.

I remember the dark-haired woman with horn-rimmed glasses in Perugia. She was looking after me while my dad went to his conference. I remember the press of her thigh next to mine on a city bus.

I remember the last steam trains I saw, train-spotting with my dad.

I remember go-karting down a street and almost being run over by a bus because I didn't want to stop.

I remember stealing cigarettes and sweets from the newsagent's after my mum and dad got divorced.

I remember throwing stones from a bridge onto the motorway until a man told me to stop.

I remember the first time I saw a James Bond film with my dad. Was that before or after he'd split up with Mum?

I remember rolling newspaper twigs to light the fire and squabbling with my sister over who should sit closest to it.

I remember learning how to knot my tie.

I remember Diana Rigg in black leather as Emma Peel in *The Avengers* on black-and-white TV.

I remember pop and crisps in the children's room at the Copt Oak Inn.

I remember the French teacher telling me off for picking my nose in class.

I remember forgetting to dry my back after a swimming lesson and the feel of my soaking shirt all afternoon in school.

I remember fish and chips scalding the roof of my mouth.

I remember running in the woods with Martin and his half-collie Jess.

I remember I was good at cross-country running, but I wanted to be good at football.

I remember I was with Martin in the woods and he said he'd teach me how to wank. He was a year older than me and knew everything.

I remember my grandma didn't like him because he had long hair.

I remember he got his girlfriend pregnant when they were both fifteen.

I remember I went to live with Martin's family on their farm when my sister died and my mum couldn't get out of bed.

I remember getting asthma from the hay.

I remember Martin took me on the back of his motorbike – a 500cc Triumph – telling me to lean with the bike when we went around a bend.

I remember being jealous of Martin's sideburns. I still hadn't started to shave.

I remember the boy with glasses who wanted to fight with me at school. I wouldn't fight someone in glasses, I told him, so he took them off and put them on the desk between us. I picked them up and put them on. You wouldn't fight someone wearing glasses, would you, I said.

I remember the boy who wanted to start a fight later gave me an original 1962 Elvis single with 'Rock a Hulu Baby' on one side, and 'Can't Help Falling in Love' on the other. It belonged to his older brother.

I remember the creepy bus conductor, who'd brush the back of his hand against a boy's arse when the bus was packed.

I remember reading *Catcher in the Rye* and wanting to drop out of school so that I could be like Holden.

I remember taking the night train on my own from Leicester to Aberdeen to see my dad. There were two men with me in the compartment who read out the dirty bits from a Mickey Spillane book.

I remember the surrealism of Philip Lamantia in *Penguin Modern Poets 13*. It wasn't like anything we were studying at school.

I remember my grandpa, who'd been a stretcher-bearer in the First World War, came to live with us after my grandma died. My mum was remarried by then.

I remember my first proper kiss with a girl. I was on a youth-hostelling holiday with Nick in the Peak District. David Bowie's *Rebel Rebel* was playing on the jukebox.

I remember going to Brees record shop in Leicester, and sitting in a sweaty booth where you could listen to one whole side of an album for free.

I remember going with Nick to see Dr Feelgood at De Montfort Hall. We hitch-hiked around the country, following them on tour. They were better than The Rolling Stones.

I remember I kept failing maths.

I remember getting drunk at the Copt Oak Inn and my stepfather shouting when I puked up at home.

I remember the sweeping rain on the first day of my 'A' levels.

I remember working in a soap factory over the summer and being frisked on the way out because someone had been stealing soap.

I remember hitch-hiking to the Lake District on my own. I discovered Henry Miller's *Tropic of Capricorn* in Windermere library.

I remember losing my virginity to Anne, a law student. She knew more than I did.

I remember getting on the bus to London with my rucksack, suitcase and adidas bag, leaving home for the first time.

I remember my mum waving goodbye.

In Memoriam Gerald

I remember writing from Italy to my dad that I'd met someone I could talk poetry and philosophy with.

I remember walking with you on Via Carlo Alberto, past the house where Nietzsche collapsed, and into the Luxembourg Bookshop, where we bought a copy of *Ecce Homo* to share.

I remember you worried because you thought I was hung up on the myth of poetic suffering and redemption. Poetry just tells another story, you said. You were a few years older than me.

I remember we took the train from Turin to Venice when they still had those compartments with leatherette seats, string luggage racks and sepia photos. It was 1983 but felt like a 1950s film, and we were starring as Beat poets.

I remember we argued over the beauty of the *Pisan Cantos* versus the politics as we sat by the canal. Like Pound, we had many lives to reconcile.

I remember we were staying with Italian friends and had to share a bed. I woke in the middle of the night, embracing you, and said, 'Sorry, I was dreaming…'

I remember the tiny tobacconist's where we bought our cigarettes to see Daniela who was behind the counter at all hours.

I remember the light in your eye, and your smile when you ordered a glass of wine. The Italian barista told me you were *ruffiano*. I thought she meant 'ruffian', but the meaning was less kind: one who deceives.

I remember you splashed your face with cold water in the mornings. Neither of us ate breakfast.

I remember the students smiled more with you than with me.

I remember the school head said it was time you grew up: you were no longer a *ragazzo*.

I remember how I hugged you goodbye at Turin station. You were returning to Venice to start a new life. It was harder than you thought.

I remember when I came to see you. You only had a single bed and let me sleep in it while you slept on a cold floor.

I remember getting lost in Paris and wishing you were with me so I'd find myself again.

I remember reading Dante for the first time and wanting to talk to you about *Vita Nova*.

I remember wandering the streets and seeing you up ahead, but when I put my hand on your shoulder, it wasn't you who turned around.

I remember later you found me on the internet and sent me poems and stories. You were ill. It was a tough gig, you said.

I remember I hadn't seen you for more than thirty years when I got the news.

I remember I was a better person when I was with you.

Last Day

In 1987, the old man who worked as a *barista* at the Caffè Elena in Piazza Vittorio Veneto, Turin, where I used to grab a coffee before work, once told me he had seen the poet Cesare Pavese the day he hanged himself in a hotel in Via Nizza in 1950. Pavese drank one espresso after another that morning in the Caffè Elena, and kept saying, 'I'm tired.'

Now when I return, the Caffè Elena is barely recognisable. Gone are the ancient smoke-stained mirrors. Gone the zinc-topped bar. Gone the greasy tables in dark corners. Now under the glare of neon light, waiters with fixed smiles serve cocktails to business people in suits.

I wonder if the old *barista* could possibly still be alive somewhere, or indeed anyone who might have seen Cesare on the last day of his life.

Fifteen Things I Learnt About

Beppe Fenoglio (1922–63), Italian Resistance Author, from Donatella C. (Museum Curator) When I Went to Visit Fenoglio's Old House in Alba and Which I Didn't Put into My PhD Thesis

1. His father, Amilcare, an atheist, ran the family butcher's from their house. His mother, Margherita, a Catholic, sold condoms under the counter.

2. As a twelve-year-old, Margherita was sent as a domestic servant to Marseilles, but wept and wept until she was sent back home.

3. Beppe often quarrelled and broke up with Luciana, his fiancée. Sometimes he wouldn't stop weeping until a mutual friend got them back together.

4. Luciana was faithful to him after he died, but not while he was alive.

5. Beppe was jealous of Cary Grant and tried to imitate him with the overcoat he wore and in the way he held his cigarette.

6. Luciana's family was much wealthier than Beppe's. She lived on the other side of the square from Beppe, the posh side. They could see each other from their balconies.

7. After the war, Beppe illegally kept hold of his rifle, pistol and British army belt, ignoring the Allies' demand that all weapons be handed over. Like many other partisans, he was ready for the call if the Fascists tried it on again.

8. But he also held on to them because he was a romantic who spent the rest of his life reliving the experience of the Resistance, including all its traumas, through his writing.

9. Beppe's role in the Resistance was a minor one, but he was the only partisan his friend and commander Piero Ghiaccio said he could rely on one hundred percent.

10. 'Schegge di bronzo' – bronze shrapnel. Not just one of Beppe's metaphors: the church bells, almost next door, are made of bronze and are ear-splittingly loud.

11. Contrary to popular opinion, Beppe was not anti-clerical. He had a deep respect for the clergy, and that is precisely why, in spite of the conformity of small-town 1950s Italy, he refused to get married in church. As a non-believer, he did not want to insult the local priest by acting hypocritically.

12. In one of the photos, Beppe and Luciana are wearing trousers and skirts made from the same material. 'Si usava molto in quei giorni.' *That's what people did in those days.* From whence the expression, 'cut from the same cloth'.

13. Donatella knows the Fenoglios well. When her phone rings, it's the author's daughter, Margherita. Giving me a complicit smile, Donatella tells her that she's with an Englishman who's come all the way to Alba for his PhD research.

14. Margherita, who works as a lawyer and who was born in the year her father died, doesn't look her age, Donatella tells me, wondering with envy how Margherita keeps herself looking so young.

15. When it's time for the museum to close, she invites me outside to smoke a cigarette. Beppe kept smoking right up until his death from lung cancer, she says, even though he wanted to stop. I gave up years ago myself, I say, leaning my face forward so that she can light the cigarette she's given me. It's cold, isn't it? she says. Our cigarettes glow in the oncoming evening.

www.ingramcontent.com/pod-product-compliance
Ingram Content Group UK Ltd.
Pitfield, Milton Keynes, MK11 3LW, UK
UKHW040746021125
464613UK00001B/33

9 781837 380114